CW00435221

Thanks a lattte

Little reminders of gratitude

SHIVANI AHUJA

All Rights Reserved.
Copyright © 2023 by Shivani Ahuja

Thanks
a
lattte

Little reminders of gratitude

SHIVANI AHUJA

"Gratitude turns what we have into enough, and more. It turns denial into acceptance, chaos to order, confusion to clarity. It can turn a meal into a feast, a house into a home, a stranger into a friend." - Melody Beattie

I'm grateful for

Mom

Dad

Shivin

Coochu

And all the dogs my mom has
adopted recently.

What are you grateful for?

- [ ] _____
- [ ] _____
- [ ] _____
- [ ] _____
- [ ] _____
- [ ] _____
- [ ] _____
- [ ] _____
- [ ] _____
- [ ] _____
- [ ] _____
- [ ] _____

Preface

Practicing gratitude every possible moment of every single day has helped me look for rainbows on stormy days. It's something that has given me hope in despair and reminded me of how identical we humans are in the midst of our vulnerability and fragility.

Being grateful for all things, little or big, is no more a practice but a mindset for me. I started my first ever gratitude journal on a hopeless dark night, when I couldn't see past the clouds of my own opinions, doubt, fear and judgments. By the time I finished journaling that night, I saw the most spectacular sunrise of my life that is vividly pictured in my mind or imprinted on my soul, as I would say. That magnificent rising sun was not just a sign of hope for me but also the most precious gift that I have treasured in my heart, forever. I hope this book can be your sunshine or rainbow on gloomy days and gives you a lens of joy to see the beauty around you.

Happy reading!

Sit back and enjoy this
toast of gratitude with a
cup of joy

Grateful for the
aroma of scented
candles

Grateful for mild
spring sun kissing
the blossoms and
reminding us of
beauty of starting
a new life

Grateful for rainbows
reminding us of
miracles after the
storms

Grateful for rain
droplets returning to
where they once
started and
completing one full
circle of life

Grateful for songs
that rewind the
clock of memories
and send us back to
happy times

Grateful for the
feeling of
accomplishment
from a successful
DIY Project

Grateful for
memories from our
favorite birthday
celebration

Grateful for
technology keeping
the spirit of love and
togetherness alive

Grateful for
parents who fail
to give up on us
even when we
are at our worst

Grateful for our furry
friends who run to
cuddle us on our good
days as well as bad

Grateful for soft,
fluffy pillows wiping
our tears off on long
lonely nights

Grateful for time
when we lose the
track of time

Grateful for games that
bring us back to good
old times

Grateful for the
things we try for the
first time

Grateful for
connections that
become deeper and
stronger with the
passage of time

Grateful for sound of thunder reminding us of the power of our voice in the most vulnerable moments of time

Grateful for lightning
warning us to leave
nature as it is

Grateful for the
moments of growth
and self-discovery

Grateful for the
most meaningful
relationships

Grateful for
the sacrifices
some of us
make to repair
our home and
restore its
beauty

Grateful for
nature that
forgives us
and bloom
again in love

Grateful for
moments we find
peace within
ourselves

Grateful for grandparents for keeping us awake with their back-to-back narration of courageous life episodes

Grateful for the
fresh air nature
return to us!

Grateful for
photo albums
we open once
in a decade

Grateful for the
'new norm' that
taught us some real
life lessons

Grateful for
our best
companions

Grateful for
finding
common
ground with
uncommon
identities of
ourselves

Grateful for the
mistakes that help
us grow

Grateful for the
sense of comfort
in our favorite
place at home.

Grateful for the
random moments
of creativity

Grateful for
little things
that fill the
voids in our
days with joy
and love

Grateful for days
we find pleasure
in non-material
possessions

Grateful for moments
when time slows
down and shows us
the magic in
boredom

Grateful for
unplanned
experiences
that surprise
us with
little
miracles
of life

Grateful for tiny
pinches of
happiness we
grab in the
passing
moments of life

Grateful for all the experiences – good, bad and worst, that eventually bring out the best in us

Grateful for clogged up plans we take for granted

Grateful for fresh meals
straight out of the
garden

Grateful for new
solutions we
find for older
problems

Grateful for
challenges that help
us uncover our
hidden strength

Grateful for
falling
snowflakes
disappearing
into magic

Grateful for the new
perspective in the
clouds of dilemma
and self-doubt

Grateful for
criticism that
adds to our list of
self reflection

Grateful for new
landscape at every
crossroad of life

Grateful for the
love universe
returns to us in
the most
unexpected
ways

Grateful for the
wishes that turn
into realities

Grateful for
the smell of
coffee beans

Grateful for healthy body,
mind and soul – teaching us
new definition of happiness
and success

Grateful for parties
where we can go
unmasked

Grateful for changing
seasons

Grateful for the
moments of laughter
with our loved ones

Grateful for wounds that
heal on their own

Grateful for
bottled-up
feelings we
finally
let

.

.

.

.

go

Grateful for living in the moments that can't be captured on our 📷

Grateful for
siblings who are
just a phone call
away

Grateful for
feeling on
letting go of
grudges

Grateful for the
beauty of a full
moon

Grateful for friends
that turned into
families

Grateful for random
messages that make
our day

Grateful for
moments when
we discover
our hidden
personalities

Grateful for the
seeds of patience
we learn to plant

Grateful for
hobbies that
make us feel
alive again

Grateful for
finding a
twinkling
star

Grateful for
moments of
solitude

Grateful for
finding our
inner child
all over
again

Grateful for diaries
that become our
closest pals

Grateful for
moments of
excitement
amidst the
adventures

Grateful for the
beauty of a
twin rainbow

Grateful for
the time we
wish we had
a pause
button
in our
life

Grateful for making a
difference in
someone's life, no
matter how small

Grateful for the most
breathtaking sunsets

Grateful for
the leap that
taught us how
to fly

Grateful for
our instincts
that lead us
through
difficult
moments in
life

Grateful for
the pieces
of puzzle
that finally
add to the
bigger
picture

Grateful for
taking a
special journey
through our
favorite books

Grateful for
both highs
and lows in
every season

Grateful for
strangers who offer
to help in the most
unexpected ways

Grateful for
the time we
feel rich
without
money

Grateful for
the lyricists
that write our
feelings

Grateful for
the pop of a
bubble wrap

Grateful for
little drops that fill
up an ocean full of
possibilities

Grateful for
life outside
of our
comfort
zone

Grateful for
delays that
help us see a
wider view

Grateful for
past-self that
lead us to the
present-self

Grateful for artists
that take us through
the miraculous
journey of their
strokes

Grateful for fearful
moments that
prepare us for
both
the best and the
worst

Grateful for
crawling into a
warm blanket

Grateful for the
smell of freshly
baked bread

Grateful for
hope that keeps
our heart from
breaking

Grateful for road
trips that turn into
lifetime memories

Grateful for fall
leaves reminding us
of beauty in letting
go

Grateful for
hot tea on a
cold snowy
day

Grateful for hot
baths that help us
unwind long days

Grateful for
the sound of
silence

Grateful for
unexpected
hugs

Grateful for smell of
fresh leaves on
misty trees

Grateful for a
perfectly ripe
avocado

Grateful for the other
side of the pillow

Grateful for
"do nothing"
days

Grateful for
luxury of
staying still

Grateful for an
aimless walk

Grateful for
simple words of
encouragement
that brightens
our days

Grateful for
warm blankets
on cold
afternoons

Coffee

Grateful for
days when our
coffee tastes
like magic

Grateful for
good hair days

Grateful for
strangers who
hold the doors
for us

Grateful for
puppy videos

Grateful for that piece of
music that brings our
emotions to life

Grateful
for little
"thank you"
notes

Grateful for
extra five
minutes of
sleep

Grateful for
passing clouds
reminding us of
temporariness in
life

Grateful for hot
chocolate

Grateful for
unplanned
vacations

Grateful for a smile from
a stranger

Grateful for fresh
flowers sprinkled
with the mist of
happiness

Grateful for the first snowfall of the season

Grateful for the
smell of rain

Grateful
for cozy
Sunday
mornings

Grateful for the
colors of sky as
the sun goes
down

Grateful for city
covered with a
fresh blanket of
snow

Grateful for the
smell of freshly cut
grass in summers

Grateful for friends
who never give up
on us

Grateful for new roads
leading us to new
beginnings

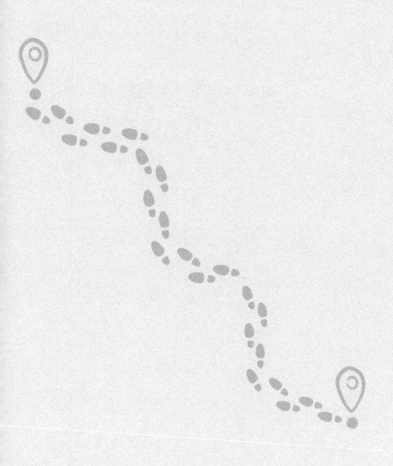

Grateful for
coming this
far!

Thank you for sipping!

Spread gratitude, sip lattes!

Share with someone you love!

I challenge you to write your
list, one latte at a time!
And send it to
youwelearn.info@gmail.com

Let's sip some lattes
together!

you_we_learn

First Published February 2023

Author: Shivani Ahuja
Publication Date: February 15, 2023

No parts of this book may be sold or copied without
the Author's permission.

To get in touch with the author, write below:
youwelearn.info@gmail.com

Printed in Great Britain
by Amazon

18160027R00086